What's Ahead ?

Transitioning
from Adult Education
to a Career

Barbara D'Emilio

Ruth Ticktin

PRO LINGUA ASSOCIATES

Pro Lingua Associates
PO Box 1348
Brattleboro, Vermont 05302 USA
Office 802-257-7779
Orders: 800-366-4775
Email: info@ProLinguaAssociates.com
WebStore www.ProLinguaAssociates.com
SAN: 216-0579

At *Pro Lingua*
our objective is to foster an approach
to learning and teaching that we call
interplay, the *inter*action of language
learners and teachers with their materials,
with the language and culture,
and with each other in active, creative,
and productive *play*.

ISBN 13: 978-0-86647-352-1; 10: 0-86647-352-1
What's Ahead? Supplement ISBN 13: 978-0-86647-353-8; 10: 0-86647-353-X

The illustrations: The following are from dreamstime.com: pages iii © Ashestosky, x © Marc Torrell Faro, 10 © Carlosphotos, 11 © Alexander Raths, 14 © Tyler Olson, 18 © Lisa F. Young, 25 © Sebastian Czapnik, 26 © Ron Chapple, 28 © Elena Elisseeva and © Daria Filimonova, 30 © Arne9001 and © Christina Richards, 35 © Dragonimages, 38 © Gregory21, 42 © Ron Chapple, 43 © Ajay Bhaskar, 47 © Monkey Business Images, 48 © Miszaqq, 50 © Del7891, 52 © Photochris, 53 © Jennifer Russell, 54 © Cmlndm, 58 © Lisa F. Young, 64 © Americanspirit, 68 © Inspir8tion. Front cover wood © Grigor Atanasov, road sign © Shahrohani; back cover day care © Diego Vito Cervo, hospitality © Dmitrijs Dmitrijevs, own business © Auremar, computer © Chiayiwangworks, skilled trades © Wally Stemberger, health © Monkey Business Images. The following are © pixbay.com: pages 3 bus, 8 learning sign, 14 electrocardiogram, 19 worker drilling, 23 analysis, 41 creativity, 44 food prep, 61 child development, 66 word ball. Other artwork: 17 CPR class by Caitlin Tromiczak – carlosrosario.org, 32 hamburger from n8tip.com, 33 © start-a-cleaning-business.com, and 51 an employment chart from the American Hotel and Lodging Institute.

This book was designed and set by Arthur A. Burrows using the sans-serif typeface Trebuchet, developed in 1996 for Microsoft by Vincent Connare; he named it for a mediaeval siege engine, because he hoped it would catapult words and ideas across the internet. Its letter forms are elegant, unusually legible, and somewhat whimsical. The book was printed and bound by Gasch Printing in Odenton, Maryland.

Printed in the United States of America
Second printing 2014 500 copies in print

What's Ahead ?

Transitioning
from Adult Education
to a Career

Other Pro Lingua books

on workplace and transition issues:

Trials and Errors

People at Work

Business Communication Strategies

For information and sample materials:

www.ProLinguaAssociates.com

Contents

To the Teacher • vi
Introduction for the Student • ix

Unit 1:   Introduction to the Workforce • 1

Unit 2:   Health Careers (*Hana*) • 10

Unit 3:   Skilled Trades (*Gamba*) • 18

Unit 4:   Your Own Business (*Tadesse*) • 26

Unit 5:   Computer Technology (*Anh Dung*) • 34

Unit 6:   Hospitality & Food Service (*Mitali*) • 42

Unit 7:   Day Care & Education (*Luz*) • 52

Unit 8:   Putting It All Together   • 62

Resources • 69

Glossary • 70

To the Teacher

What's Ahead? is designed to address the needs of intermediate- or advanced-level students but can be adapted and used in differentiated classrooms. Our goal is to provide students with vocabulary, information, and skills related to a variety of careers where job growth is expected in the 21st century. We hope that the insights and skills your students develop working with this material will enable them to move on to various courses that prepare them for certificates, licenses, and degrees in the fields covered in the text or others that may interest them. As you review this book, keep the following in mind:

1. This is a flexible text, not a script. Feel free to adapt it to fit your teaching style and your students' specific needs and areas of interest.

2. The text is an excellent companion to books you are using that focus on grammar, reading, and other aspects of language learning.

3. Use students as resources. There will be many students who will be able to talk from experience about the various workplaces and careers discussed in class. Use them to enrich the discussion and learning experience.

4. Spend time at the beginning of each class to review student work, answer questions, and address specific grammatical concerns.

5. It is helpful to do part of the class in a computer lab so that students who may not have access to computers for the research activities will be able to work on them and receive help.

6. Daily writing reflections are encouraged.

7. When possible, invite guest speakers, show videos, DVD's etc. Students may be helpful in identifying speakers.

8. Accompany the text with additional readings pertinent to your local situation. Our students read, discuss, and write about a variety of reading selections.

9. Some students' writing is included in this text as examples for your students.

10. Also check page 69, Resources, for internet listings that may help you learn more about the careers and skills in this book or to find useful supplementary material.

We have pilot tested this curriculum over the past three years at a community college, in an adult ESL charter school, in local classrooms, and at workshops at WATESOL and non-profit organizations. Revisions have been made based on these experiences. We look forward to your input as you use this text.

- Barbara & Ruth

The Supplement for *What's Ahead?*

Although it is not necessary to have the supplement, it can be a very valuable tool for enhancing the students' learning experience. You can download the supplement for free from Pro Lingua's website (address below) by clicking on the book cover on the home page, or purchase the 30-page supplement separately. The following information and copyable material is contained in the supplement.

- Description of the purpose of each section of each unit
- Brief teaching notes for each unit
- Copyable one-page Review/Assessment for each unit
- Answers to the exercises in this book
- Appendices, including
  "The Job Board" - a copyable page with a variety of job titles
  EFF (Equipped for the Future) *Readiness Profile* - shows which
    work skills are covered in each unit
  Copyable Career Survey/Questionnaire to help students focus
    on career choices
  A copyable list of *Additional Readings* that support
    critical thinking skills

To download: (www.ProLinguaAssociates.com)

Acknowledgements

This book is an outgrowth of the expressed needs of our diligent,
inspiring students who are working hard to fulfill their dreams.

We are grateful to the students, teachers, and staff of
Carlos Rosario International Public Charter School,
Washington, D.C., www. carlosrosario.org and of
Prince George's Community College,
University Town Center, Hyattsville, MD, www.pgcc.edu,
for their inspiration and interest in this book.

And our special thanks to the student writers whose writing
enriches this book.

What's Ahead?

Welcome to **What's Ahead?** The book includes activities that draw on the information and skills you bring to the classroom. You will enhance this knowledge, develop your on-the-job communication abilities, learn self-assessment and how to identify employment opportunities and career goals, complete a résumé, and practice interviewing for a job. These skills are applicable to all employment and educational situations. As you work on them, you will continue to develop listening, reading, writing, speaking, as well as problem solving, critical thinking, researching skills, and the ability to work in teams.

This book also introduces you to careers in the areas of hospitality, health, skilled trades, computer technology, entrepreneurship, and education/child care. There is job growth today, in the 21st century, for these careers. Learning about them will help you pursue your educational goals and choose a career.

Vocabulary development is an important aspect of all the work in this book. There are stories and readings throughout the book, and before many of them you will see instructions to look for and underline certain words in the story or reading. These are words you need to know as you think about careers and the world of work. Be sure you understand them. If you do not, ask your teacher or look in the Glossary on pages 70 to 78 for simple definitions.

Unit 1
Introduction to the Workforce

Tapping into what you know

As a way to begin working with your classmates, think about a job you had in the past. What did you do? Who did you work with? What skills did you bring to your job? What did you like and dislike about your job? Share your thoughts with a partner or small group.

Look for and underline these words in the story

to apply, to reject, to accept, troubled, a retirement community, elderly, eventually, to advance, to wonder, to complain, an electrician, a skill, determined, a goal, to upgrade

Story: *A Bus Ride*

It is a cold, snowy evening in Riverdale. In the darkness, a group of people wait for the bus to take them home after a long day of work. Many of them left home before the sun came up. They get on the bus, find a seat, and relax. There is time to think.

Mitali, a young man from India, sits in the back of the bus. He has been in the U.S. for almost a year. He wanted to go to England where his sister lives, but he won the visa lottery to come to the U.S. Since his cousin lives in Washington, D.C., he went to stay with him. Mitali was a good student and graduated from high school in India. He is 19 years old and has not had much work experience. He thought he'd find a good job as soon as he got to the U.S. After applying for many jobs and being rejected, he finally accepted a job as a dishwasher in a big hotel. He doesn't know exactly what he wants to do in the future, but he doesn't want to wash dishes all of his life. He wonders what it would be like to work as a cook in a restaurant. Mitali is tired and troubled. His name means "friend" in Hindi, and right now he could use a friend. "What can I do to get a better job?" he asks himself.

Hana, an Egyptian woman in her 40s, is waiting at the bus stop in front of her friend **Tadesse**'s grocery store. She likes to support Tadesse, an Ethiopian man in his 50s, by doing most of her shopping at his corner store. She carries two heavy packages as she waits for the bus.

Hana came to the U.S. seven years ago with her three children after her husband died. She started out working two jobs – one as a housekeeper at a retirement community and the other as a server at a restaurant on weekends. She is now working as a home healthcare assistant with the elderly. She is good at her job and wants eventually to become a nurse. Her name means "happiness," and she brings happiness to the people she helps. To advance in her job she needs to get her Certified Nursing Assistant (CNA) certificate. As she waits for the bus, she thinks about how she will get that certificate and wonders if she knows enough English.

Hana remembers the hard times Tadesse went through before he got his store. Tadesse, whose name means "renew," has always found a way to start again despite the many challenges he has faced. He encourages other members of his community, like Hana, to learn English and take advantage of every opportunity. By following his example, Hana believes that if she works hard she will succeed.

Gamba from Cameroon, a 30-year-old man with lots of energy, gets on the bus. His co-worker **Luz**, from Nicaragua, is with him. They sit near the driver and talk about their jobs as cashiers at a big department store. They complain because they are bored working as cashiers. Gamba was an electrician in Cameroon and really liked that type of work. He wants a job as an electrician here and the opportunity to learn new skills, too. Luz was a teacher in her country. She loves children and is a great storyteller and math teacher. She really wants to teach again. Gamba, whose name means "warrior," is determined to reach his goal to be an electrician and upgrade his skills. Luz, whose name means "light," wants to continue her work as a teacher, to bring the light of education to children in this country. "What do we have to do to use the skills we had in our countries here in the U.S?" they ask.

Anh Dung gets on the bus in front of a laundry/dry cleaners. She is 50 years old, from Vietnam, and on her way home to the apartment that she shares with her family. Her sister brought her to the U.S. two years ago. In Vietnam Anh Dung had worked as a receptionist in an office. She began to learn about computers and now wants to study computer programming. Her name means "strength," and Anh Dung is strong-willed and determined to be successful in this country. "I am willing to work and study a lot to reach my goal," she thinks to herself.

The bus is not only transportation to and from work but a place where people think about their troubles and give life to their hopes and dreams.

Understanding the story

1. What jobs did the riders on the bus have before they came to the U.S.?
2. What skills do they have?
3. What are their goals in the U.S.?
4. What do they need to do to reach their goals?
5. What advice would you give Mitali who is young and without much support from his family?

Word study

Fill in the blanks in the following sentences using these words.

applied, wonders, complain, accepted, upgrade, eventually, rejected, advance, retirement, elderly, troubled, skilled, goal, determined, electrician

Example: Her sister **brought** her to the U.S. two years ago.

a. Mitali _____ for many jobs but was _____.

b. He _____ a job as a dishwasher.

c. Hana works at a _____ community with the _____.

d. She wants to _____ in her job and _____ become a nurse.

e. Gamba and Luz _____ because they are bored with their jobs.

f. Gamba wants to _____ his skills.

g. Hana _____ if she knows enough English.

h. Ahn Dung is _____ to be successful. She will work very hard to

   reach her _____ of being a computer programmer.

i. Gamba was an _____ before he came to the U.S.

j. Mitali is _____ because he doesn't know what to do.

k. _____ workers know how to do their jobs well.

Look for and underline these words in the reading selection

supplies, a temper, diplomacy, a customer, a relationship, to manage, expenses, stock, rewarding, a character, to deceive

Reading selection: A Past Job

During all my childhood I helped my parents with their grocery store. We sold supplies to our neighbors, and from this station of my life I learned to control my temper and my tongue: diplomacy. Also, my parents taught me that in order to get a successful business one must think of the customers and build a relationship with them. This knowledge was the foundation of my own business later, but it wasn't all I needed to know. I had to learn to manage money, when to spend and when to cut my expenses. I learned about stock, what to buy, how many and at what time. Dealing with people was the hardest and at the same time the most rewarding thing of that whole experience. During my childhood I knew all the people, but later as the town grew, many new people arrived so when I had my business, many times I had to judge people's character. This taught me how people can deceive in order to get what they want.

Written by a pre-college student

Discuss the reading

1. What did this student learn from her parents?
2. What lessons have you learned from your job?
3. What was the most difficult part of this student's job?
4. Do you think the writer is too negative about people?
5. Talk about an experience where you used diplomacy or wished you had.

Writing

Think about "A Bus Ride." Write about yourself. What job are you doing now? What would you be wondering about if you were on your way home from work on the bus one evening?

Skill building: knowing yourself

It is important to set goals for the future. In order to reach your goals you need to know yourself, the things you do well, and those things you want to do better. Developing this skill is known as self-assessment.

Strong Points & Weak Points

Strong points, or strengths, are things that you do well. They can also be character traits that make you suitable for a career. Strengths are your selling points. You talk about them at your job interview and describe them on your resume.

Consider the following words that describe strong points:

adaptable	*good leader*
hardworking	*self-confident*
cooperative	*creative*
reliable	*deliberate*
dependable	*precise*
team player	*intelligent*
quick learner	*organized*

Weak points, or weaknesses, are things you do not do well. It is important for you to know these things so that you do not take a job where you may not do well or that you will not like. If you work best when you have time to think about your tasks, you may not want a job that is very fast-paced. While working slowly may not be appropriate in some jobs, there are many jobs that value someone who is deliberate and thoughtful.

Weak points may be strong points on another job.

Consider the following weak points:

I don't work well with a lot of noise
I like precise directions
I am not a leader

Using skills

Think about yourself, your past jobs, characteristics, likes and dislikes.
Make a list of your strong and weak points.
Now, ask two people who know you to read your list.
Do they agree with you or have anything to add?

STRONG POINTS	WEAK POINTS
_____	_____
_____	_____
_____	_____
_____	_____
_____	_____
_____	_____
_____	_____

Adapted from www.executive-and-life-coaching.com/support-files/
smartgoalsettingworksheet.pdf

Research

Choose a partner and interview each other in order to find out what skills your partner has from previous experiences. Ask your partner what their ideal job would be. Complete the chart on the next page with your partner's responses.

The following questions can serve as a guide:

1. Where are you from?
2. What kind of jobs did you have previously?
3. What skills do you have?
4. What do you do well?
5. What do you like to do?
6. What do you dislike doing?
7. What kind of job would you really like to have?

Job Likes & Dislikes

In a recent job my partner liked	Partner disliked

Previous skills	Partner's ideal job

Look at the chart your partner filled out for you. Think about your strong points and weak points. Then think about your ideal job and make a list of the skills you think you will need on that job. Compare these skills with the skills you have now.

Unit 2
Health Careers – CNA and EMT

(Certified Nursing Assistant and Emergency Medical Technician)

Tapping into what you know

Brainstorm names of jobs related to health care that you know about from your experiences as a consumer of health care.

Look for and underline these words in the story

nutritious, wise, patient, medication, vital signs, cancer, dementia, terminal illness, basics, geriatric, a registered nurse, success

Story: *Hana*

I came to the U.S. seven years ago from Egypt. I have been in the U.S. for seven years. My three children and I came to Washington D.C. to live with my brother and his family after my husband died. My husband and I owned a restaurant near Cairo. I learned a lot about taking care of people, managing a business, and making nutritious food. Now I work as a home health care assistant. I love my job because I take care of the elderly. In my country the elderly are respected and honored because they are wise and have much to teach us. They live with their families until they die.

In the U.S. the elderly are often put in nursing homes to be taken care of by others. I like being able to take care of them. I help my patients take a bath and make sure they have nutritious food. I remind them to take their medication on time and I go with them to their doctors' appointments. But I want to do more. I want to be able to provide first aid and to understand their vital signs, illnesses, and medication. I want to help them deal with cancer, dementia, and terminal illnesses. I plan to learn the basics now, get my Geriatric Nursing Assistant (GNA) Certificate and continue in college and become a registered nurse (RN). I want my children to know that it is never too late to learn something new, to advance, and to reach your goals. Learning is the key to success.

Understanding the story

1. What career is Hana interested in pursuing? Why?
2. What will she be able to do in her chosen career?
3. What is her goal?

Word Study

Try to match the job titles in the first column with the job duties in the second column. Write the correct letter from the Job Duties column on the line provided in the Job Title column. Discuss your answers with your classmates.

Job Title	Job Duties
___ Certified Nursing Assistant (CNA)	*a* draws blood and transports blood samples
___ Dental Assistant	*b* provides advanced medical treatment at the site of an injury and crisis intervention
___ Geriatric Nursing Assistant (GNA)	*c* schedules patients, manages medical records, provides basic patient care
___ Registered Nurse (RN)	*d* works with the elderly
___ Pharmacy Technician	*e* checks vital signs, and provides pre-hospital emergency care for patients, often works with fire department or on ambulences
___ Phlebotomy Technician	*f* helps patients with health care needs such as feeding, bathing, and dressing
___ Medical Office Assistant	*g* prepares the patient for the dentist, washes and sterilizes instruments, and assists dentist
___ Emergency Medical Technician (EMT)	*h* works under the supervision of a pharmacist, providing medicine by filling prescriptions and providing health care products to patients
___ Paramedic	*i* supervises CNA/GNA's, assesses patient needs and plans for patient care with the doctor, gives medication

Look for and underline these words in the reading selection

a bruise, fractured, a wound, a splint, a cast, stitches, crutches, unconscious, CPR, a pulse, a splinter, tweezers, relieved

Reading selection

What a busy day I have had! I am an EMT Basic. I work with firefighters and help them respond to emergencies in the community. Today we went to a car accident on Georgia Ave. We treated a woman who had many bruises, a fractured leg, and a deep wound on her arm. We put cold packs on the bruises, put a splint on her leg and stopped the bleeding in her arm and bandaged it. We took her in the ambulance to the hospital where they put a cast on her leg and put stitches in her arm to help it heal better. She was very upset, but I stayed with her until her family arrived. I also helped her learn how to use crutches.

When I got back to the fire station we received another call. A woman called to tell us that her elderly father seemed to be having a heart attack. When we arrived he was unconscious. We applied CPR* until his pulse and breathing returned to normal. We took him to the hospital where he had an operation.

It was a long day. When I got home my daughter was crying because she had a splinter in her finger. I got the tweezers and removed it and put a band-aid on it. I was relieved that it was a minor problem.

* cardiopulmonary resuscitation

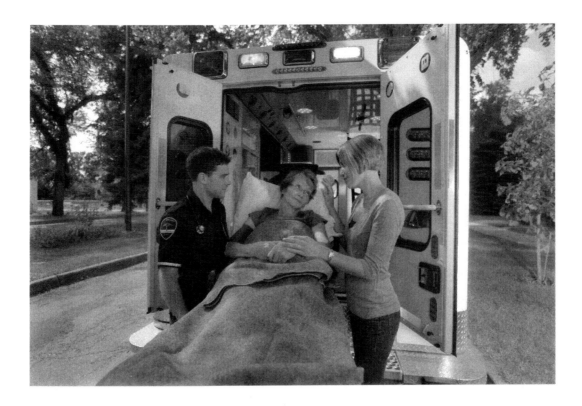

Discuss the reading selection

1. What do people working as EMT Basics and in other nursing related careers have in common?
2. How are their jobs different?
3. What skills do people entering health careers need?
4. Why is work in the medical profession a good choice?

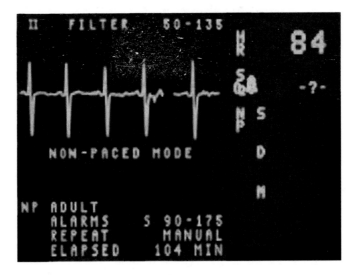

Writing

Choose a health career that you are curious about. What does a practitioner in that career do, and why it is interesting to you? Write about it.

Read the following selection about a hospital emergency.

It was about 3:00 a.m., and I was sleeping when the phone rang. I woke up half asleep and I picked up the phone. My friend answered in Spanish and said, "I'm Marisol. I'm so sorry to bother you at this time."

I said to her, "Don't worry. Do you need something?"

She said, "Yes."

She was crying and so I asked her, "What's the problem?"

She said, "I need you to go to the hospital with me to translate into English."

I said, "OK, Let's go. I'll wait for you outside."

I hung up the phone and I didn't ask her for more details. I dressed as soon as I could and I went out to wait for her. In a few minutes I saw her husband's car coming. I got in the car and then I started to ask her what was wrong.

She said, "I don't know why but I have had a big pain killing me all night."

I said, "Oh my God, how come?"

She said, "I don't know. I just ate an order of fries with a chicken sandwich and a bottle of water last night."

We arrived at the hospital emergency room at about 3:30 am. I registered her and we waited until about 7:00 am. The nurse called her and asked her the reasons why she was there. So Marisol told me in Spanish about the pain that she was feeling. I repeated it in English to the nurse.

The nurse told me to ask her if she had had any symptoms similar to her pain before.

Marisol said, "No, it started last night. It was a big pain from the back and moved to the left."

The nurse sent her to a small bed to wait for the doctor. A half hour later the doctor came and examined her. He asked many questions again about the pain and told her to wait. She had a kidney stone. After that, the doctor gave her two prescriptions; one for pain and one to help move the kidney stone along. We left the hospital at 12:00 noon: she took the medications and never felt that pain again.

written by an ESL student

The health professionals asked additional questions of the patient.
What other questions would you add from your own personal experience?

Skill building: communication

Whether you go to a clinic, a doctor's office, or the emergency room, you will be asked the following basic questions in addition to filling out a medical history form:

What's the matter?

Where does it hurt?

How long have you felt like this?

Are you taking any medication?

What kind of medical insurance do you have?

Using skills

In groups of three, choose one of the following role plays and practice your communication skills. Read the scenario and choose characters. Act out the scenario and present it to the class.

GROUP A - Roles to be played: mother, child, and nurse at a clinic in the community. Choose a health problem for the child. The mother goes to the clinic and explains the problem to the nurse. The nurse questions the mother and child to find out more about the child's symptoms. Then the nurse helps the child.

GROUP B - Roles to be played: EMT, 911 Operator, and a person with an emergency problem. A person has an emergency problem (you choose; it could be chest pain, a broken leg, etc.). The sick person calls the 911 Operator who asks questions about the person's problems. She sends out the EMT to the person's home. The EMT arrives, asks questions to find out more about the problem. The sick person answers. The EMT checks vital signs and helps the person.

GROUP C - Roles to be played: Pharmacy Technician and two people who are sick and want help. One person is the Pharmacy Technician working at a pharmacy and two people are sick (one has a prescription) and want to ask for help. You decide what the problems are and act out the scene for the class.

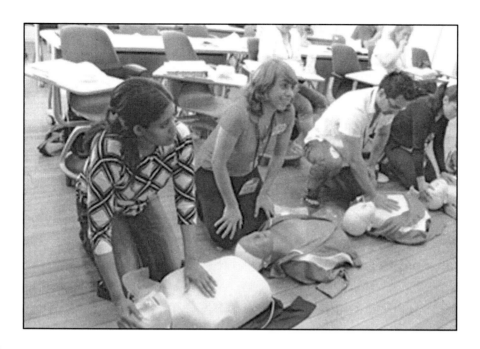

Research

Choose one of these or another health career for a presentation at the next class.

EMT	CNA/GNA	Dental Assistant
Phlebotomy Technician	Pharmacy Technician	Medical Office Assistant
Massage Therapist	Radiology Technician	Physical Therapist
Occupational Therapist	Fitness Trainer	Nutritionist
Medical Assistant	Home Health Aide	Lab Technician
Practical Nurse	Nurse Practioner	Physician's Assistant

Imagine you are a practitioner of that career. Tell the class, in the form of an oral or written story, about the work you do. Include the following in your presentation:

1. the name of the career
2. what the person does in this career
3. skills they need for this career
4. educational qualifications.

You can gather this information by talking to someone in this health-related career. You can also research these or other jobs in health care on the internet. Check out these career websites:

> www.acinet.org/acinet/explore/View.aspx
> www.careerinfonet.org

While other students are presenting, take notes of anything of interest to you or any questions you have for the presenter.

Unit 3
Skilled Trades and Green Jobs

Tapping into what you know

Imagine that you won money in the lottery, and you want to build a house. Write your responses to these questions and share them with the class.

Who will you call?

What will the house look like?

What kind of workers will help you build the house?

Look for and underline these words in the story

an appliance, to repair, an architect, blueprints, a plumber, a carpenter, a contractor, a welder, a glazier, a bricklayer, a crisis, a counselor, a fuel, to construct, to pollute, the environment, harmony, strategies, an apprenticeship, to install, solar panels

Story: *Gamba*

My name is Gamba, and I am from Cameroon in West Africa. As a child in my country I liked to take things apart and to put them back together. My father owned a repair shop and I helped him fix household appliances, like toasters, blenders, and other things. I eventually became an electrician, repaired electrical problems in homes, and helped put electricity in new houses. I saw how the architects' blueprints were used to guide the building of the new houses. It was so interesting that a piece of paper could turn into a building.

I liked working as a part of a team. I was able to meet many talented people: builders, plumbers, carpenters, architects, contractors, welders, glaziers, carpet installers, and bricklayers, who make it possible for people to have homes. I thought my life was secure but because of a crisis, I had to leave my country. I cannot work as an electrician here because I do not have a valid license.

During the last local election I heard a lot of talk about creating green jobs. So, I decided to find out what they are and to see if I could get one. I went to a career counselor to find out about green jobs. We discussed how the fuels and materials we use for transportation and to construct, heat, cool, and light buildings, and many other things have polluted our environment. Green jobs are being created to help us live in harmony with our environment and stop polluting it. The counselor suggested strategies for obtaining green jobs and told me I could go for training at a community college adult education center, and possibly get an apprenticeship.

I have decided to go to classes to learn how to increase energy efficiency in buildings by installing solar panels and energy-efficient windows. My dream is to be part of a group that builds a school for children that is good for our environment.

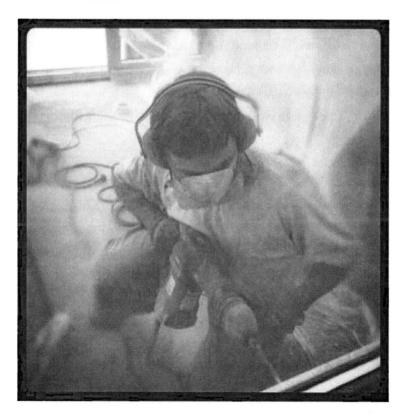

Understanding the story

1. What was Gamba's career in his country?
2. Why was he interested in the career he chose in his country?
3. Why isn't Gamba practicing his career in the U.S?
4. Who did Gamba talk to about green jobs?
5. What are green jobs?
6. What kind of job does Gamba want?

Word Study

Skilled Trades

Fill in the blanks using the following words:

plumber, bricklayer/brick mason, electrician, painter, HVAC* mechanic or installer, roofer, welder, carpenter, glazier, contractor

1. _____ a person who agrees in a contract to do a certain job, such as building a school, or remodeling a bathroom

2. _____ a person who installs glass in windows, skylights, walls, or store fronts

3. _____ a person who installs or repairs heating, central air conditioning, or refrigeration

4. _____ a person who heats and puts together two or more pieces of metal so that the finished piece is strong

5. _____ a person who paints the outside and inside of buildings

6. _____ a person who builds or repairs roofs

7. _____ a skilled person who fits and repairs the pipes of gas and water systems or appliances

8. _____ a person who installs, maintains, and repairs electrical wiring, equipment, and fixtures

9. _____ a person who lays and binds building materials, like brick or cinder block, with mortar to build or repair walls, etc.

10. _____ a builder or repairer of wooden structures or objects

* Heating, Ventilation, and Air Conditioning

Look for and underline these words in the reading selections

to preserve, to restore, conservation, an expenditure, toxic, to/a retrofit, hazardous, landscaping, weatherization, composting, precipitation

Reading selections: *Green Jobs* and *Weatherization Technician*

Green Jobs

What are they?

Green jobs are work force opportunities in agriculture, manufacturing, research and development, administration, and services that preserve, protect, and restore the quality of the environment. They are often blue-collar jobs that are performed in ways that benefit the environment such as zero waste, energy and water conservation, recycling, low or no carbon expenditure, no toxic inputs.

What specific types of jobs exist today?

- car and truck mechanic jobs related to biodiesel or alternative fuels
- energy retrofits to increase efficiency and conservation
- green building construction
- hauling and reuse of construction materials and debris
- hazardous materials clean-up
- landscaping
- non-toxic household cleaning in residential and commercial buildings
- solar installation
- whole-home performance, attic insulation, and weatherization
- water retrofits to increase water efficiency and conservation
- small businesses producing products from recycled materials
- parks and open space expansion and maintenance
- green waste composting
- bicycle repair and bike delivery services
- printing with non-toxic inks and dyes
- tree cutting and pruning
- urban agriculture
- recycling and reuse

Why are they important?

Green jobs restore and protect all aspects of our environment and also assure the health and safety of workers, communities, society, and the planet itself.

Weatherization Technician, a student's perspective
by Norma Suriel

Manuel filed his taxes this weekend and one of the questions on the form was "Occupation." Manuel decided to write "Weatherization Technician," even though he knew there would be many questions from the person who was helping him file his taxes. The volunteer, who was typing the information in the computer, asked him:

"Weatherization Technician? What do you mean?"

Manuel was waiting for that question. Almost everybody asks, and Manuel, who loves his job, always gives a very long explanation about it.

"First of all, you need to know what weatherization is," Manuel said. This was the beginning of a very long conversation.

"Weatherization is the practice of protecting a building and its interior from the elements (particularly from sunlight, precipitation, and wind), modifying a building to reduce energy consumption, and optimizing energy efficiency."

"I have never heard about that," said the volunteer.

"That's because it's a new trade. The U.S. Department of Energy provides funding to states by the Weatherization Assistance Program. It enables low-income families to permanently reduce their energy bills by making their homes more energy efficient. And at the same time they are creating new jobs," explained Manuel.

"O.K. So your job is related to the green revolution and global warming. It's a green job," added the volunteer.

"Actually it is. The energy conservation resulting from the efforts of states and agencies helps our country reduce its dependence on foreign oil, and decreases the cost of energy for families in need, while improving the health and safety of all the homes."

"Wow! Your job is very interesting. And what are some of your duties, like what do you do on your job every day?" asked the volunteer.

"Well, I install insulation, apply sealing materials, and make repairs to reduce energy losses. I hang and adjust doors for a tight fit, caulk and glaze windows, seal rim joists and top plates, repair roof leaks, wrap water lines, and install attic and wall insulation using special equipment," said Manuel.

"And what kind of education or qualifications do you need for this job?"

"Just a high school diploma and, of course, a Weatherization Certificate."

"What skills do you need?" asked the volunteer.

"Experience with building construction, carpentry, and basic computer skills," answered Manuel.

"I see you get a good wage," the volunteer continued. "O.K. Manuel, I've finished. Do you have any questions?"

"No. Thank you for all of your help," said Manuel.

"It was really nice to work with you. I've learned a lot through our conversation. Thanks and have a good day."

Discuss the readings: *Green Jobs* and *Weatherization Technician*

1. What are examples of jobs that protect the environment?
2. How could you retrofit your home to be more energy efficient?
3. What comes to mind when you hear the phrase "global warming"?

Writing

You are part of the group working with Gamba building and installing systems for an energy-efficient school. Pick one of the construction occupations and describe some of the aspects of your work on this project.

Skill building: Problem Solving

Figuring out how to solve problems effectively is an essential skill for all careers. It is particularly important in construction, where failure to solve a problem properly could lead to accidents or unsafe buildings. The five-step method for solving problems gives you a way to look at problems and find solutions effectively. It also gives you confidence in your ability to address problems in all areas of your life.

1. <u>What is the problem?</u>
   Describe exactly what the problem is. Be clear and specific.

2. <u>What is my plan?</u>
   Think of at least two or three possible strategies that you might use to solve the problem. A strategy is a way, method, or process for solving a problem. It's not the solution itself, but it shows how you can find the solution.

3. <u>What might happen if?</u>
   Examine your list of possible strategies and consider possible outcomes. Choose the one that seems best.

4. <u>Try it out!</u>
   Try your best strategy and see if it works to solve the problem. If it works, you're done!

5. <u>How did I do?</u>
   If your best strategy doesn't work, go back to your list of possible strategies in Step Two and choose another. Then, try it.

Or, stop thinking about the problem for a while, and come back to it later.

Or, research the problem, and then start again with Step Two.

Adapted from www.gttp.org/html/canadalinks/curriculum/AppendixA.html
Canadian Travel and Tourism 5 Steps to Solving a Problem

Other tools for solving problems

Brainstorming
Get together with a group and spontaneously make a list of suggestions.

Pros and Cons
Write the pros and cons of one possible solution and weigh them for effectiveness.

Root Cause Analysis
Ask five "why" questions about the problem to determine the specific causes of the problem.

Cause and Effect Diagram
Draw a picture of the problem's cause and effect.

Flowchart
Draw a map showing the steps in the process of solving the problem.

Using skills

Choose one of the problems below and solve it with a partner. When you have a solution, ask yourselves what tools you used to solve the problem. Then present the results to the class.

PROBLEM 1

You arrive home and find your basement apartment full of water. A pipe is leaking. What do you do? Who will fix it and what tools will be used?

PROBLEM 2

A hurricane hits your city and knocks the roof off your house and breaks the windows. What do you do? Who will help you fix it? What tools will be used?

PROBLEM 3

It is a snowy day. You arrive home and there is no heat in your house. What will you do? Who will you call on for help? What kind of tools will they use?

Research

Manuel mentions certification in green jobs. Look up one of these certification programs. Write about it, defining and explaining the training for this type of job.

Home Builders Institute, a residential construction academy – www.hbi.org

Energy Practitioners – www.nabcep.org/certificates/entry-level-certificate-program

Building Performance, for HVAC, contractors, auditors – www.bpi.org

Green Advantage, for contractors and trades – www.greenadvantage.org

National Assn Home Builders, certified green professional – www.nahb.org

Remodeling Industry's "Green Certified Professional" – www.nari.org

Build it Green Professional – www.builditgreen.org/cgbp

Leadership in Energy and Environmental Design – www.gbci.org or www.usgbc.org

Unit 4
Your Own Business

Tapping into what you know

Think about a business you are familiar with that is successful. What makes it a success? What are the components of a well-run business? Now think about a business that is struggling. What do you think needs to be done to turn it around?

Look for and underline these words in the story

expectations, chaos, to flee, permanent residency, finance, merchandise, maintenance, regrets, an opportunity

Story: *Tadesse*

Tadesse's family in Ethiopia had very high expectations of him. He was to finish high school, go on to the university to study economics, and then get a good job like his father, who worked at the post office in Addis Ababa. However, at the time that Tadesse was studying at the university, there was chaos in the country. The government was changing, there was fighting in some areas, and the economy was very bad. Tadesse felt that he had to flee the country and was, therefore, not able to complete his university studies.

A friend helped him come to the United States where he met and soon married Algainesh. Tadesse wanted very much to become a member of his new community in the U.S. He was thrilled when he finally obtained his permanent residency. He was determined to improve his situation and have a career in business. He also wanted to continue his studies in finance. But, first step first, he had to improve his English language skills, and find work.

After a few jobs that he didn't really like, Tadesse was hired at a neighborhood market. He got to know and like the customers and learned about ordering merchandise and store maintenance. When the owner of the market retired, he offered to sell the store to Tadesse, who had saved enough to buy it. Tadesse and Algainesh work seven days a week at the store.

Asked if he had any regrets, Tadesse answered: "I feel very fortunate to have this opportunity. I work hard, but I am my own boss. I continue to learn a lot about business, so I think I have met my expectations."

Understanding the story

1. Why did Tadesse flee Ethiopia?
2. What did Tadesse want to study at the university?
3. Describe the kinds of things Tadesse deals with in his business.
4. Why does Tadesse feel that he has met his own expectations?

Word Study

Use the following words to fill in the blanks in the story below:

chaos, finance, permanent residency, proud, expectations, merchandise, maintenance, regrets

Mrs. Cruz received _____ _____ in the U.S. five years ago. She worked hard to get the skills and money to buy and operate a business. She felt so _____ to own her own business. Mrs. Cruz hired an employee who had high _____ for himself, but he needed a job to support his growing family.

She arrived at the store early one morning and found it in a state of _____. The window was broken, rain had come into the store, and much of the _____ had been thrown onto the floor. She called her son, Mario, who was getting a degree in _____. He came and asked neighboring store owners for help. The owner of the fast food place asked his _____ person to help Mrs. Cruz and Mario clean up the store. She _____ what happened but feels lucky to have such good neighbors.

Another Business Model: Cooperatives

Look for and underline these words in the reading selection

wages, challenging, leadership, consensus, wages, a client

"We Can Do It"

An interview with Luz M. Hernandez

What is "We Can Do It"?

"We Can Do It" is a women's cooperative business. We clean people's houses and offices.

What is a cooperative?

A cooperative is a business that is run by the workers. We make the decisions. We support each other. We work together as a group, and we are getting to know one another. It's the best thing that has ever happened to me.

How did it start?

We were in an ESOL class in Brooklyn. We wanted to work. Some of us had jobs, but our employers did not always treat us fairly. We wanted a cooperative so we could get fair wages and make our own schedules. The people at the community center told us that we could create a cooperative business. If we worked as a cooperative business, we could have living wages and flexible schedules.

Do you have leaders?

We don't have leaders. We have a leadership committee. The committee changes every year.

How do you make decisions?

Sometimes, some of us have ideas. We talk about the ideas, and we go forward with the best ideas. Usually, we agree by consensus that an idea is good, but sometimes we decide by voting.

What do you like best about working in a cooperative?

I work fewer hours, I meet different people, and the clients treat us better. Also, I like to work in a group. I like to listen to the other members.

What is most challenging about it?

The challenge is to get more work for the members of the cooperative that need it. Another challenge is to find more time to spend with our children.

How is your cooperative being affected by the economic crisis?

Some of our members do not have as much work. They have to look for new clients.

What does the cooperative do if the member does not have work?

We try to share the clients so that everyone has work. We also look at why someone is losing clients. Maybe the clients are not happy because the work is not being done well. In that case, we try to help the worker do a better job.

Are you in an English class?

Yes, I am taking an English class. It's important to study English, if you have the opportunity. For me, it's very difficult because sometimes at work I can't express myself well, and I would really like to express myself well.

How do you find time to study English?

I get support from my husband. He takes care of my daughter when I go to my English class.

Look for and underline these words in the reading selection

demolition, to abuse, a hazard, to integrate, independent, discrimination

"We Can Fix It"
A Worker Cooperative that Does Repair Work and Has No Bosses
An interview with Victor Rodriguez

 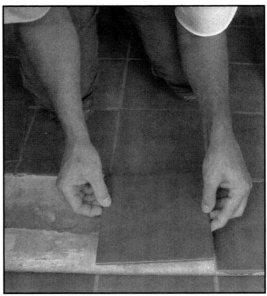

What is "We Can Fix It"?

"We Can Fix It" is a cooperative of men and women. We do small construction jobs and repairs. The cooperative is a support for us as immigrants. We do demolition, repairs, painting, and sanding floors. We have experience hanging sheetrock and fixing holes in plaster walls and ceilings.

Why did you set up a cooperative? Why not an ordinary business?

We wanted a cooperative so that our salaries would be fair.

What was it like working in construction before you were in a cooperative?

I had to walk the streets looking for work. The bosses abused the workers. Sometimes I got paid. Sometimes I didn't. I had to have my own tools. They did not give us protection from hazards on the job. When I was working with hazardous materials, I had to push my boss to give me a mask or something to cover my mouth.

How has being in a cooperative affected other parts of your life?

We are learning how to run a business. We are integrating ourselves into society. I feel like a person who can do important things.

What do you like best about working in a cooperative?

We are independent because we are our own bosses and workers. And we don't have to give information to any bosses or anybody, only to the members.

What is most challenging about it?

Not speaking perfect English. Sometimes we ask the adult educators at the school for help.

Is your cooperative being affected by the economic crisis?

Yes, it is being affected. There are not enough jobs.

What sort of support does your community need?

It is important for community centers and schools to give workshops so that day laborers and immigrants know their rights. Some don't know their rights, and they are suffering discrimination.

*From **The Change Agent**, September 2009*
Author is a student at Center for Family Life, Brooklyn, NY.

Discuss the reading

1. What is a cooperative and how is it different from Tadesse's and Mrs. Cruz's businesses?
2. What do you learn from working in a cooperative?
3. What are the advantages to working in a cooperative?
4. What are the disadvantages?

Writing

Write about a cooperative or a small business that you would like to start in the future. Answer some of the following questions:

- What kind of company will it be?
- Why are you starting it?
- Who will get involved in the ownership and management?

Skill building: constructive criticism

The ability to work well with people is a critical skill for any job. It is particularly important in a business where you have to deal with other employees as well as customers. On the job, one encounters many situations where it's necessary to offer criticism that will help the other person work more effectively.

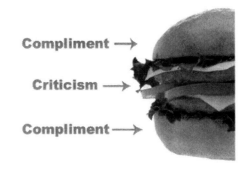

Compliment →
Criticism →
Compliment →

Here's a method used for offering "critical" advice to another person: It's called the hamburger method, and here's how it works:

1. When offering criticism, you begin with a constructive compliment about something the person does well (otherwise known as the fluffy bun part).

2. You then get to the meat of the matter, which is the constructive criticism part where you offer the person advice on how they can improve.

3. Finally, you end with another constructive compliment (the other half of the fluffy bun). Basically, you're sandwiching the constructive criticism between two constructive compliments.

from http://n8tip.com/the-hamburger-method-of-constructive-criticism-works-for-vegetarians-too

Using skills

Now think of an example where you could use the hamburger method. For instance in the reading about the "We Can Fix It" cooperative, if one member of the team arrives late, the customers will be inconvenienced and the work of the group could be viewed negatively. One of the members of the cooperative might say: "I'd like to give you some feedback on your work. You are a talented carpenter and work well with us." (the compliment) "But you do not arrive on time and this causes problems for the other workers and our customers. I would like you to make an effort to arrive at least five minutes before we have to leave for the job." (the area that needs improvement) "I want you to know how much we value your commitment to the cooperative and how much we want you to continue working with us." (constructive compliment)

In pairs, practice using the hamburger method of compliment and constructive criticism to deal effectively with a work-related problem. Choose a situation where you would like to offer constructive criticism. Then practice with your partner.

Research

Look for and underline these words in the passage below

an innovation, market research, competitive analysis, a business model, financial projections, a team of managers

---

How do I start my own business?

First, I have a business idea, an innovation, that I need to assess to see if it is a good idea. I check out the need for this business and do market research. I compare my idea with other similar businesses in a competitive analysis. I write up exact specifics of how the company will operate – that's the business model. I decide what expenses I will have, and what money I will make – that's the financial projections, and I put together a great team of managers to help run the business.

Take the business idea you wrote about previously, or think about other business careers like real estate, marketing, accounting, or legal services. Begin a formal plan. Use the business plan above or other links you find for small business startups.

Some questions to ask yourself

1. What is new about my business idea?
2. What is my competition?
3. Where do I do the market research?
    4. Who shall I get to be involved in the ownership or management?

Unit 5
Computer Technology

Tapping into what you know

Choose a question and discuss it with another student. Then share your discussion with the whole class. Finally, as a group, talk about attitudes towards technology.

Would you go out with someone you had met over the Internet? Why or why not?	What invention do you think has had the greatest impact on society? Why?
Do you have an e-mail account? What do you use it for, and how often do you use it?	What do you think the world will be like in a hundred years?
Do you think that people will ever visit or live on other planets?	In what ways has technology improved our lives? In what ways has it made life worse?
Imagine that you could own only ONE of the following: a computer, a cell phone, or a car. What would you choose and why?	How has the Internet changed what you do every day?
Are there some things that never should have been invented? What are they and why?	Could you work from home with a computer?
How "real" will virtual reality become?	How has technology affected the way we fight wars?
Do computers save or waste time?	How much of a risk are computer viruses?

Adapted from www.eslpartyland.com/teachers/conversation/cqtech.htm

Look for and underline these words in the story

a widow, to export, a computer technician, software, to troubleshoot, a disaster, bankrupt, laid off, to postpone, to raise

Story: *Anh Dung*

I am from Hanoi, Vietnam, and I'm the oldest of six children. I finished secondary school but never got to college because my mother died, and I had to work and take care of my brothers and sisters. I quickly learned how to listen, communicate clearly, solve problems, and work hard. All of my brothers and sisters have finished school, married, and started families. I found a good husband, but he was killed in a bus accident.

After I recovered from the shock of becoming a widow, my luck changed and I got a very interesting job as a receptionist at an export company. They treated me well, and the computer technician taught me how to use computers. I really love doing things on the computer and learned how to install software and to troubleshoot some problems. I thought another disaster had hit me when the company went bankrupt.

A week after I was laid off, my sister, Kim, invited me to live with her and her family in Virginia. She has a good job and offered to pay for me to go to school to improve my English and to become a computer technician.

That was four years ago. I have studied hard, I obtained my green card, and I am getting certification to become a computer technician. I realized that I had a lot of the skills for becoming a good technician because I raised a family at a young age and because of my work experiences in Hanoi. I communicate well with people and am a good listener so that I understand the problems people are having with their computers. I am a good problem solver and a patient troubleshooter. Since I understand how computers work, I am able to help my coworkers solve their computer problems. So, at age 50, I feel like I am starting a new life. My sister, Kim, says that she is giving me the life I postponed when I raised my brothers and sisters many years ago. It is never too late to learn. You just have to stay strong and have hope.

Understanding the story

1. What skills did Anh Dung bring with her to her new career?
2. Why are those skills necessary for work in technology?
3. How do you feel about the last two sentences of the story?

Word Study

Match the words with the definition

_____ widow	a.	to take care of children until adulthood
_____ export	b.	change an event to a later time or date
_____ computer technician	c.	unable to pay debts
_____ install	d.	to deal with serious problems, investigate
_____ software	e.	fired because of a company's financial problems
_____ troubleshoot	f.	to put into a computer
_____ disaster	g.	a woman whose husband has died, and who has not remarried
_____ bankrupt	h.	a business of selling goods to another country
_____ laid off	i.	a person skilled in operating and fixing computers
_____ raise	j.	the sets of programs that tell a computer how to do a particular job
_____ postpone	k.	a sudden event such as an accident, flood, or storm that causes great harm or damage

Look for and underline these words in the reading selections

IT, a photographic memory, oral, geeks, an administrator, an engineer, to highlight, an operating system, an intern

Reading Selections

Four interviews in the field of information technology: **A Computer Technician, A Computer Engineer, A Network Associate, A Computer Teacher**

A Computer Technician

"What can you tell me about the career of a computer technician?"

"I'm new to the computer or IT field. The only training I got for the A+ certification exams is from a career college. On the tests, I remember there being hardware, software, and basic networking questions. Networking is communicating within a group. It took 90 minutes to complete, and I passed. I earned a diploma in Computer Networking from the school and my A+ certification. The training and classes were very good and easy for someone wanting a career in IT and who has a photographic memory like me. Right now, I'm trying to get a job as a computer technician with only the A+."

"So what other certifications do you need?"

"I need MCSE certifications. When you pass one MS cert, you are automatically an MCP (Microsoft Certified Professional). To be an effective computer tech, it depends on the quality of the schooling you took, how experienced you are as a computer technician, how good you are as a computer technician, and your certificates.

"To be a very good computer technician, you need to have good oral communication and people skills, great computer skills, be a good listener, a good problem solver, and a patient troubleshooter. There are a variety of career paths one can take after getting experience as a computer tech. Three or four years of being a computer tech with the MCSE can help you get a really good paying System or Network Administrator job. Overall, you have IT experience over the other 200+ new geeks (computer nerds) who have applied for that System or Network Administrator position, because you got your start in the IT field as a computer technician."

Adapted from www.indeed.com/forum/job/Computer-Technician/ best-computer-technician-qualifications-training-get/t6643 photo

A Computer Engineer

I interviewed Paul, a computer engineer, and I found out that his role is quite varied. He must complete a multitude of tasks in his daily work environment. The following will highlight this career as well as list some of his responsibilities and duties.

Paul told me that he has an important job in the world of technology. The basic definition of a computer engineer is one who researches, plans, and develops computer operating systems. He says that he uses his knowledge in the field of computer science, math, and engineering to ensure that he carries out his daily job tasks to the best of his ability.

He said, "I have several general responsibilities that I have to do in my job. I research information about computer operating systems, review the current system, maintain it, and make changes to the system." Sometimes he develops operating systems of a certain type. Paul does a lot of work maintaining the current operating system and checking the system to make sure everything is working correctly. He has to monitor his work and fix any problems connected to the operating system that come up. Also, he has to maintain contact with a large number of individuals, customers, project managers, and other company employees.

These are some highlights of his career and examples of his duties and responsibilities as a computer engineer. "There can be a lot more to this job," Paul said.

Student writing by Juan Guevara

A Network Associate

His name is Chris and he is from Virginia. He has been working for the same organization for four years. What he likes is the challenge and the fast-paced action. Sometimes he has to work long hours. About the career of a computer technician, he thinks it is a job that never ends. Even when he is on vacation, he's still working.

Five years ago he got a certificate as CCNA (Cisco Certified Network Associate). There are many kinds of certifications. For him the most difficult work is building the computer. He really likes computers. This is one of the skills people need to be involved in for this career. Also he is a problem solver and a patient person. He has good communication with people. Because of these skills, Chris is a successful computer network associate.

Student writing by Leticia Guzman

A Computer Teacher

An interview with Janett Arandia, who came from Bolivia ten years ago. Her current job is as a teacher for a computer literacy class at an adult ESL school.

Q. "Why did you come to the U.S.?"
A. "I was looking for better opportunities in my life. I was feeling like my home was too small for me. Also, I was feeling that my dreams were just dreams and never a reality."

Q. "Why did you decide to be a computer support specialist?"
A. "...For different reasons. One reason was the challenges, because not many women were studying that career and of course I wanted to have better income. Since everything now is related to technology, I fortunately had the opportunity to start that career at school."

Q. "Are you planning to study and get more certifications in the future?"
A. "Yes, that is one of my goals."

Q. "Did you have some experience as a computer technician?"
A. "In the beginning I did not have any experience or knowledge at all. Everything was new for me, but now, I feel more confident because of the training that I have had, the experience as an intern, and the assisting and teaching jobs in the computer field."

Q. "How do you feel about this new career, and is it different from the previous experience and knowledge that you had?"
A. "I feel like I have more or better opportunities, even though it's not related to the previous career that I had. I believe that everything that we learn will help us to be prepared for new challenges and opportunities in our lives."

Interview conducted by a student

Discuss the four reading selections

1. Why is the field of study called information technology?
2. What are some of the skills and characteristics common to all of the computer jobs discussed in the readings?
3. Do you think computers will increase the number of job opportunities or replace jobs?

Writing

Develop your own list of questions about the IT field and interview someone you know who works in computer technology. Make sure you include questions about their training and current and future job prospects. Share your stories.

Skill building: creative thinking

In Unit 3 we introduced the five-step method for problem solving, a process of thinking about solutions to problems. An equally valuable way of thinking is called creative thinking. It is the ability to come up with new ideas by combining them, changing them, or using an old idea in a new way. A creative person

- is curious
- welcomes problems as interesting opportunities
- likes to be challenged
- is optimistic
- lets go of judgments for a while
- does not give up easily
- is not afraid to make mistakes, because you can learn from them.

In this unit, Anh Dung used creative thinking when she did not give up after she became a widow or when she lost her job. Instead, she thought about the skills she had developed raising her sisters and brothers – attentive listening, clear communication, hard work, the ability to solve problems – and she saw that she could reapply those skills to the work of a computer technician.

It is important to remember that we all use creative thinking, especially as children and with children. It is critical to bring this type of thinking to the workplace in these times when we are being challenged by rapid change and technological advances.

Adapted from virtualsalt.com/crebook2.htm

Using skills

Imagine that you are part of a group of computer technicians at an organization that is considering a change from desktops to laptops. You want to make a proposal that will be cost-effective and efficient for all departments.

Decide as a group how you will go about this change. Describe what you propose to do so that the managers will be convinced that it is a good idea. Make sure you combine your ideas, make necessary adaptations, and/or use something that already exists in a new way.

Make an outline of your proposal, or any other creative idea for change that you have, and present it to the group.

Research

Companies provide training in this field in addition to academic training. Review these links:

> www.microsoft.com/learning/student-career/en/us/career-job-role-chart.aspx

Consider the job titles in this unit as well as web designer, developer, and computer analyst or specialist. Look at the Microsoft curriculum roadmap.

> www.microsoft.com/learning/education/roadmap

What career path would you take, and why?

Unit 6
Hospitality & Food Service

Tapping into what you know

Fill in as many jobs as you can think of in each of these three aspects of the hospitality industry.

Lodging	*Restaurants/Food Service*	*Recreation/Travel/Tourism*
_____	_____	_____
_____	_____	_____
_____	_____	_____
_____	_____	_____
_____	_____	_____
_____	_____	_____
_____	_____	_____
_____	_____	_____

Look for and underline these words in the story

to yell, stressful, to worry, to store, a prep cook, a reference, culinary arts, a chef

Story: *Mitali*

My name is Mitali, and I am from India. I am not happy with my job as a dishwasher at the hotel. My supervisor yells at me a lot and tells me to work faster, which makes the job stressful. And I don't have health benefits, which worries me as I wonder what will happen to me if I get sick. The good thing about my job is that while I am washing dishes I get to see what happens in the kitchen. I watch what the cooks do and sometimes, on my break, I help out by chopping vegetables and storing food when the deliveries arrive. I am learning a lot about food service.

Since I have no family here I have to cook for myself. I try out what I learn in the hotel when I am at home. It's fun. I really think I want to be a cook in the future. Now I am looking for a job as a prep cook in a restaurant that provides health benefits. The cook I help at the hotel offered to give me a reference for my next job. I also found out that the community college offers courses in the culinary arts. I have many dreams for the future. I could open my own restaurant, or maybe I could get a job as a chef for an international hotel and travel to many different places. They even need chefs at the White House. The possibilities are endless.

Understanding the story

1. Why doesn't Mitali like his job as a dishwasher?
2. What kind of job is he looking for now?
3. What kind of work does he want to do in the future?
4. What are some possibilities Mitali has not considered?
5. What kind of courses does the community college offer?

Word Study

Fill in the blanks using the following words from Mitali's story.

to yell, stressful, to worry, to store, a prep cook, a reference, culinary, a chef

1. _____ a person who is the main cook

2. _____ to shout or say something very loudly

3. _____ a person who is willing to speak about your skills and character to future employers

4. _____ to place or leave something (food) somewhere (refrigerator)

5. _____ a person who prepares food for the main cook to use

6. _____ to think nervously about someone or something

7. _____ concerning the kitchen or cooking

8. _____ full of or causing tension, unrest, imbalance

Look for and underline these words in the reading selection

lodging, options, typically, to transfer, initiative, a quality, a personality, an appearance, demanding, to exceed, a facility, competitive

Reading selection

Choosing a Career in the Hospitality Industry

So, it is time to decide what you will do with your life. What will you choose? Perhaps you might consider a career in the hospitality industry. What is the hospitality industry? The hospitality industry is defined as the activity of providing lodging, food service, and recreational services, which include but are not limited to hotels, motels, clubs, casinos, restaurants, recreation facilities, tourism, cruise lines, and theme parks. What a variety of options! As a multibillion-dollar industry, hospitality is our country's third largest industry, employing nearly 9.5 million people nationally. The possibilities are many, but what does this mean for you?

What career options are offered in the hospitality industry? Where do you start? What types of careers are available? These are the major questions to consider when pursuing a career in the hospitality industry. The following descriptions outline the different levels of hospitality positions you might enter into.

Entry-Level: This is where you start; the experience and skill you will gain in these positions can prepare you for advancement in your career. Typically the tasks are quite simple, and do not require a lot of previous experience.

Skilled-Level: This is the next step where you can develop specific skills that can be *transferred* from one position to another (you are on your way).

Managerial-Level: This is when your experience, training, and initiative give you the ability to lead employees and manage a business.

The following are specific career opportunities at the managerial level of the industry:

LODGING Hotel/Motel General Manager, Meeting/Conference/Sales Manager
FOOD & BEVERAGE Restaurant, Club, Kitchen, Bar, and Banquet staffs
RECREATIONAL Resort Manager, Tour or Travel Consultant

As you can see, you have many choices, but what qualities must you possess? The hospitality industry, like many other industries, requires a certain personality.

To be successful, you must
- like people, be a hard worker
- have strong communication skills, be willing to sacrifice
- maintain a professional appearance
- have "common sense"
  (be able to think on your feet, respond to guests' needs)

What are some additional qualities?

Although these qualities may seem simple, they are often put to the test by the people you serve in this very demanding industry. No matter where you work in the hospitality industry, you will be required to exceed expectations to make sure the experience people have at your facility is valuable, pleasant, and memorable.

Once you obtain a position and work hard, what can you expect to be paid? Today, wages for the hospitality industry are very competitive. Compared to those of other industries, a wide range of salaries is available.

Lastly, remember your career decision must be YOUR choice. A career in the hospitality industry can be very rewarding and exciting, and will afford you the opportunity to travel and work with thousands of people. Every day is different from the previous day.

Adapted from www.studydiscussions.com/how-to-choose-a-career-in-hospitality-industry/photo

Discuss the reading selection

In pairs or small groups, answer these questions and report back to the whole class.

1. What is the main idea of the article?

2. What kinds of careers can you find in the hospitality industry?

3. What is the difference between entry-level, skilled-level, and managerial-level positions?

4. What skills do people in the field of hospitality need?

5. What do you know about being banquet or catering managers, pastry chefs, restaurant owners, or travel agents?

Writing

Customer service is an important part of all of the careers in the hospitality industry. Read the following story and think about your experiences with customer service.

Greeting Customers

Talking a lot is not for me. I remember when I started to work at the Gap. The Gap is a clothing store, so we depend on customers and how we treat them. At the beginning I didn't talk to the customers, because I wasn't comfortable talking to them. I only spoke if they asked me questions about sizes, colors, or styles. Renee, my manager, saw that, and of course she talked to me about it. I was folding clothes near the fitting rooms and she came next to me. She told me, "I'm happy with you. Actually all the managers are happy about your work." But the problem was that I was too shy. Renee said to me, "You need to talk to the customers and greet them."

So I started little by little, greeting the customers, and now I'm so happy because she gave me great constructive criticism. Now I do a better job with the customers and I'm not scared or shy to talk with customers.

Written by an adult education student

Write about an experience that you had as a worker or as a customer in a restaurant, hotel, or airport. It can be a story of a positive and helpful encounter, or a misunderstanding. Share your story with the class.

Mitali Goes on a Job Interview

Five years have passed since Mitali got a job as a dishwasher. He has taken courses in the culinary arts at a community college and has worked as a prep cook for two years. Mitali eats at a small restaurant in his neighborhood every Sunday. Recently he found out that the cook is leaving. He decided to apply for the job. The owner of the restaurant, Ben, interviews him. They greet each other and sit down to talk. Let's listen in!

Ben: Tell me about yourself, Mitali.

Mitali: I came to the U.S. five years ago from India. I have been working in the hospitality industry since I arrived. I have completed courses in the culinary arts program at the community college. In my current job at Riverview Retirement Community I have worked as a prep cook for the last two years. My supervisor often lets me take her place as a cook when she is not able to come to work. *I now have enough experience and knowledge to become a cook*.

Ben: Why do you want to work here?

Mitali: I really like this restaurant. I eat here every Sunday because the food is so delicious. Since I know the menu here I am sure I would be able to do a good job *and even expand the menu*.

Ben: What are your strengths?

Mitali: I am hard-working. I learn quickly. I get along well with co-workers and customers. I am honest and reliable. I am also flexible. I can stay late or come to work early when you need me. ***I will run an organized, safe, and clean kitchen***. I like to work as part of a team.

Ben: What is your greatest weakness?

Mitali: I am a quiet person but I have found that being quiet often makes other people in the kitchen calm when things get busy.

Ben: What are your career goals?

Mitali: I want to continue studying and ***eventually open my own restaurant***.

Ben: Do you have any questions for me?

Mitali: How many hours a week will I work?

Ben: You will work 40 hours a week. We pay for overtime.

Mitali: How many people will I supervise?

Ben: You will supervise the five people who are on the kitchen staff. Can you cook a meal for me tomorrow so that I can see if you will fit in at my restaurant?

Mitali: I would be happy to.

Using skills:

1. Look at the underlined phrases in the interview. Were these good statements for Mitali to make?

2. After critically analyzing the statements that Mitali gave in the job interview, offer other suggestions.

3. Critique your experience at a job interview that you had.

4. Review your answers in Unit 1 about your strong points and weak points. Then practice interviewing each other.

Boat tour of the Chicago River

Research

Look at the illustration from the American Hotel and Lodging Association that includes wages for various careers. With the picture in mind, think of some related careers that we have not yet explored.

Examples are: event, meeting, or party planners, tour escorts, operators, and guides, travel agents, airline personnel, caterers, bartenders, public relations and sales personnel and managers.

Research one of these or other careers in this industry. Choose one of interest to you, and use a variety of resources to investigate and describe the job and specific functions. Tell your classmates the advantages and disadvantages of this career.

Typical Hospitality Career Ladder

Climb the Ladder to Success

A career in hospitality offers your students an exciting professional future that allows them to put their goals, interests, and abilities to good use in a field with limitless potential.

Controller
$90,000

General Manager
$89,400

Catering Director
$81,000

Executive Chef
$76,500

Director of Marketing and Sales
$74,500

Director of Human Resources
$74,100

Director of Security
$59,100

Front Office Manager
$51,000

Sales Manager
$50,000

Convention Services Manager
$48,000

Executive Housekeeper
$46,200

Assistant General Manager
$45,000

Sous Chef
$34,300

Line Cook
$25,000

Front Desk Associate
$21,800

Housekeeping Attendant
$19,200

Information based on 2011 Survey provided by WageWatch, Inc.
888-330-9243
Please note that the salaries reflected for the lodging industry are the median average rate and each position has the potential to earn a higher salary.

American Hotel & Lodging Educational Institute

12-04200
32073X DM04ENGE

Courtesy of the American Hotel & Lodging Educational Institute

Unit 7
Day Care and Education

Tapping into what you know

Think about the skills your favorite teacher had. Make a list of the skills you think are necessary to be an effective child care provider or teacher. Share your list of skills with your classmates and highlight those that everybody has listed.

Look for and underline these words in the story

a co-worker, to long, moved, a child care center, increasing, to arrange, folks, a toddler, valid, senior staff, a requirement, approved, registered, to demonstrate, excited

Story: *Luz*

Luz was on her lunch break at the large discount store where she works as a cashier. She met her co-worker, Ellen, who was also on break, and they decided to eat together. As they sat down, Luz said that she was a kindergarten teacher in Nicaragua, and that she really wants to work with children here in the U.S. She had tears in her eyes as she explained how much she longs to work with children again. She thought Ellen might be able to help her because she is from the U.S.

Ellen was very moved by her co-worker's desire to return to teaching. Suddenly she had an idea. Her cousin, Marian, runs a family child care center in her home and has many Latino families who want to bring their children there. Since Marian is increasing the number of children at the center she will need more staff, especially someone who speaks Spanish and English. Ellen called Marian on her cellphone and arranged for her to meet Luz.

They met at Happy Folks Family Child Care Center, where Marian takes care of 12 children from toddlers to ages three and a half. She interviewed Luz to find out her qualifications. Marian was not sure if Luz's qualifications from Nicaragua would be valid in the U.S., but she could definitely hire her as an assistant teacher. For Luz to be part of the senior staff she would have to meet some requirements, such as a number of hours of approved training, some college credits, and supervised work experience at a preschool or registered family child care center. It could take a year.

Luz spent a day volunteering at Happy Folks to demonstrate her ability to work with children. After Marian had seen her work with the children, she asked Luz how much she was making as a cashier. Marian decided to pay Luz the same amount to work as an assistant teacher. Luz was very excited because she realized that this work experience at Happy Folks, along with the required classes she planned to take, will make it possible for her to become a senior staff member. She was on her way to getting back into teaching, with the realistic hope of eventually becoming a teacher in the U.S. Maybe she will even study early childhood education or elementary school education in college.

Understanding the story

1. Why did Luz have tears in her eyes when she talked to Ellen?
2. What was Ellen's idea and what did she do about it?
3. Who did Luz meet with and what did she find out?
4. What requirements does Luz need to be a senior staff member?
5. Why was Luz excited?

Word Study

Write sentences using one of these words in each sentence:

toddlers, a requirement, approved, child care centers, to arrange, to demonstrate, to increase, valid

1. _____

2. _____

3. _____

4. _____

5. _____

6. _____

7. _____

8. _____

Look for and underline these words in the reading selection

to explore, observations, to interact, intrigued, instinctive,
to discipline, confidence, manipulatives, continuity, consistent, thrived

Reading selection

Reflections of a Preschool Teacher

If you are considering a career in early childhood education (teaching or assisting in a school for young children), or if you are a parent thinking about what school would be best for your child, it is important to explore what goes on in a preschool.

Josie Etheart, a Haitian-American who has been an educator for 30 years, talked with us about her experiences and offers some observations. She was happy to share her thoughts about teaching, and what she had learned over the years about early childhood education.

Josie liked to babysit as a teenager and volunteered at a day care center in high school because she had fun and learned from interacting with children. While in college she visited a trilingual day care center and was intrigued and thrilled by the fact that the children were spoken to in Creole, Spanish, and English. Soon afterward she was hired as a teacher there. She explained that day care centers are usually open from 8 a.m. until 6 p.m. They should be set up to promote the best in child development but also provide overall care, such as meals and nap time. It is a convenient place for working parents to leave their children while they are earning a living.

Josie eventually went on to work in preschools that also offer a child development program similar to day care centers but are open fewer hours, usually half a day, or until 3 o'clock at the latest. She thinks that both are valuable resources for children and their families.

While classes in early childhood education that teach child development theory are helpful and some training is definitely necessary, Josie believes that much of what a teacher does is instinctive and comes from the heart. Teaching requires being comfortable with children and feeling passionate about helping them see and understand the world so that they are able to find their place in it.

A preschool teacher is an actor, stage director/drama coach, science teacher, art facilitator, psychologist and counselor, music facilitator, nurse, and more. A teacher also has to know how to take on the role of authority, set limits, redirect and discipline children, and also be willing to sweep the floor, wipe noses, clean tables, and do other jobs that aren't glamorous.

One day an adult woman walking with a young girl approached Josie with a big hug. She told her former teacher how important she had been in her life, and that she realizes the importance of good teachers now that she owns her own successful small business. She tells her nine-year-old daughter (the young girl at her side) that school can make you who you are and be the key to your success. She is a living example of the power of a good teacher's influence on her students.

The ideal classroom invites boundless discovery and free exploration. A variety of areas that are pleasing to the eye encourage the students to play creatively with building blocks, to explore music, math, and science through dramatic play, and to develop confidence and a love of books. The art area has plenty of easels, materials for art projects, old recycled objects to build with, and anything that inspires imagination. The block area is often next to the dramatic play area to encourage interaction between the areas. There are also areas with books, musical instruments, and CD's, and one with manipulatives such as Legos, Duplos, puzzles, pegboards, and small building items. Water and sand tables are necessities in the preschool classroom. In an effort to provide more opportunities for exploration and discovery, teachers will occasionally fill the sand table with potting soil, beans, or flour.

Most of the time, the children should be free to choose the activities in which they want to participate. While they have a lot of freedom, the teachers are present to ask and answer questions that further the learning process, and to help the children deal with conflicts and frustrations. "Circle time" offers opportunities for the children to come together and interact as a group. Here they learn songs or poems, talk about problems, learn about time, the seasons, and counting, or read a book together. The days are scheduled so that the children know what to expect at different times, and therefore have a sense of continuity and predictability. A typical day includes arrival, free play, circle time, story time, snack, outdoor play, and departure for home. The classroom is a world within itself that mirrors the world outside. The seeds of curiosity, exploration, imagination, and understanding oneself and others are planted in the preschool classroom and grow as the child does.

It is not only the child who is learning and growing. Josie describes teaching as a process of mutual discovery and development. This collaboration among teachers, co-workers, supervisors, parents, and children builds a strong community. Josie remembers one of her most challenging students, who cried every day for weeks. With patience, allowing the child to cry if necessary, and by collaborating with the parents so that home and school were consistent, the teacher helped the child become accustomed to the school and thrive there.

Josie learned the value of working with parents, who are such important resources to the school. Parents should be welcomed and encouraged to contribute their talents and skills to the schools. Grandparents and guardians are often involved in the ideal classroom as well.

Josie's years of experience have taught her that it is important to work at a school that is in agreement with your beliefs about child development. It should be a place that helps all children thrive, develop the skills they need to contribute to the world, and respect the rights and feelings of others. By doing this, preschool teachers contribute daily to building a better world for all of us. It is a career worth pursuing, one that changes lives, both the teacher's and the students'.

Discuss the reading selection

1. What are some of the choices a good preschool teacher offers in the classroom, and why are they essential for the children?

2. What are some things that are necessary for safety and health that a child has no choice about? Give some examples of when teachers may need to assert their authority.

3. Why is it especially important for the teacher to involve parents when a child is having problems at school?

4. What do you do if you don't know the answer to a child's questions?

Writing

There are many kinds of teachers. School teachers are the ones we are most familiar with, but family members, neighbors, and peers are also valuable teachers. Write about a time when someone helped you reach an important life goal. Why was that teacher important to you?

Skill building: understanding course requirements for postsecondary education credit or certification courses

In order to establish yourself in a career you will need to take required coursework depending on your choice of careers. The schedules of classes from local post-secondary schools such as trade schools, community colleges, or universities list the coursework needed to obtain a certificate or degree. Once you are enrolled in a class you will receive a syllabus, which is like a roadmap of what to expect from the course: course description, objectives, assignments, projects, due dates, evaluation, and school polices. A syllabus helps you make sure that the course meets your needs and expectations.

Using skills: understanding a syllabus

Read the following syllabus from a child development course.

Child Development Course Syllabus

(sample)

One-semester course, for example, 3 hours a week for 15 weeks

Instructor's name:
    Room #:
    Phone number #:
    Email address:
Office Hours:

Course description:

This course addresses knowledge and skills related to child growth and development from prenatal through school-aged children, equipping students with child development skills. Students use these skills to promote the well-being and healthy development of children and investigate careers related to the care and education of children.

Course objectives:

Students will demonstrate understanding of processes, theory, practice, scientific methods, etc.

Materials needed for class:

Textbook (name, author, & publisher), notebook, folder, plus access to website:_____

Evaluation/Grading Procedures *(example)*:

The grade is determined in the following manner:

** 30% of the grade will be composed of daily work, article reviews, papers, presentations, and small projects.
** 70% of the grade will be composed of major exams that cover units of work.

A student will be responsible for obtaining and completing any makeup work in a satisfactory manner and within the time specified by the teacher.

Attendance and School Policies:_____

Some courses include a clinical component and observation by the instructor that is part of the grade.

Some states require a transcript from this type of class in order to grant licensing of a day care center.

Upon completion of this and additional coursework, you can obtain your CDA, Child Development Assistant Permit.

Child Development Course Syllabus
(page 2)

Course Outline and Assignment

Date	Topic	Assignment Readings
	Overview/Theories	
	Research Methods	
	Biological and Environmental Foundations and Interactions	
	Prenatal Development	
	Birth and Newborns	
	Exam (oral and written)	
	Infancy growth and motor skills	
	Learning and perception	
	Piaget/Article Review due	
	Information processing language	
	Emotions	
	Observation paper due	
	Information processing language	
	Emotions/self	
	Gender parenting/child maltreatment	
	Exam	
	Physical development	
	Information processing/ADD	
	IQ/Languages/School	
	Observation paper due	
	Self/emotions	
	Moral development/peers	
	Review/Final Exam	

If you are more interested in another career, get a syllabus from a friend who is attending a class in that field of study or use a syllabus from a class you are taking now, or ask your teacher for a course syllabus relevant to your needs.

After reading the syllabus, discuss it with the class.
Make sure you use the following words:

objectives, an evaluation, policies, grading procedures, an overview

Research

Choose one of the following;

1. Interview a teacher.

   • How and why did they become a teacher?

   • What are the best things about being a teacher and what are the most difficult?

   • Write a summary.

2. Become familiar with early childhood education certificate options, both credit and non-credit.

   • Get a copy of your local community college's schedule of classes.

   • Investigate the meaning of: Non-credit; Credit; Child Care Certification; A.A. Degree; B.A. in Education.

   • Are there mandatory classes in: child growth and development; curriculum development; health, safety, and nutrition; professionalism; and special needs?

   • What are some of the other courses?

   • What are similarities and differences in the programs?

Unit 8
Putting It All Together

Tapping into what you know

Make a list of the jobs you learned about in each of the fields below.
Put a star by the ones that you want to investigate further.

Health	Skilled Trades
Business	Education
Hospitality	Computer/IT

Look for and underline these words in the story

to ponder, elementary, dead-end, eager, an audience, emotional, ecstatic

Story: *An End and a Beginning*

Eight years have passed since the people on the bus were pondering their futures. Luz is an elementary school teacher who works with many students who are speakers of other languages. She knows that for her students to succeed, their families must be actively involved in their children's education at home and work as partners with the school.

Parents often tell her they are struggling to find employment or are working in dead-end jobs when they are capable of so much more. She remembers being on the bus. Luz wants to do something to help them and decides to organize a career night for families.

Luz called her friend Gamba to see if he would help plan the career night and be one of the speakers. He was happy to get involved and agreed to talk about green jobs and how to apply for them. The city had just put more money in the budget to weatherize government buildings and to optimize energy efficiency in a variety of ways, so there will be many employment opportunities in the near future. Luz and Gamba decided to put a request for volunteer speakers on a community website, or list serve that is widely used. Before long a chef named Mitali had contacted them, eager to talk about his restaurants. A computer engineer named Anh was willing to talk about careers in IT. Hana, a nurse who had recently started her own home healthcare business, said she would be happy to talk about her journey from Certified Nursing Assistant to Registered Nurse. Tadesse and Algainesh wanted to speak to young parents about how they saved money and worked hard to finally buy their own store. They would proudly describe how they had improved and expanded the business carefully over the years.

Luz and Gamba interviewed the speakers, clarified their audience's interests and needs, and gave them guidance on their presentations. Each one of the speakers talked about how much they had struggled to achieve their goals and how honored they felt to be able to help someone in a similar situation. The date was set. Luz asked her colleagues to provide child care, and Mitali provided food for all of the participants and their families.

As Luz watched the speakers take their places in the front of the room she became emotional. She was ecstatic that she had exceeded the dreams she had when she was on that bus so many years ago. But she was even more overcome with emotion because the work she was doing with children and their families would probably transport them to a brighter future. She wiped the tears from her eyes and the program began. Algainesh smiled as she held her firstborn grandchild in her arms. Tadesse whispered in the baby's ear: "la anta, for you."

Understanding the Story

1. What does Luz believe the parents should do to help their children succeed?
2. What happened at career night at the school?
3. How did she find the volunteer speakers for the event?
4. What do you think Tadesse meant when he whispered, "la anta, for you" in the baby's ear?

Word Study

Write eight sentences using the following words:

to ponder, elementary, dead-end, eager, an audience, emotional, ecstatic

1.

2.

3

4.

5.

6.

7.

8.

Look for and underline these words in the reading selection

to pursue, an obligation, a majority, an obstacle

Reading selection

The teacher in an Adult ESL class, who was very impressed with her students' progress and abilities, asked the class: "What has kept you from returning to school to earn a degree or upgrade your skills?"

A few students responded: "I'm not sure what degree I should pursue," or "My English skills aren't good enough yet." Some students said that the problem was "I have too many family and work obligations," or "Covering the cost of tuition is too difficult." The majority of the students answered: "I have been out of school for too long." That surprised the teacher, who understood some of the other obstacles.

It was after this discussion that the teacher decided to help the students become more confident about their abilities. He pointed out that they all were able to read, understand, discuss, and write about the material covered in class. The teacher also emphasized that learning is a lifelong process that they are already participating in by taking their studies seriously. He encouraged them to believe in themselves and their abilities to succeed as lifelong learners. Then he taught them a chant:

> "We can do this, oh yes we can.
> Look, we managed, we made a plan,
> And step by step we climbed and ran,
> Made our dreams real, oh yes we can."

Instead of focusing on what might hold them back, the students are looking forward to the future.

Discussing the Reading Selection
1. What are the obstacles holding you back from upgrading your skills?
2. What does it mean to be a "life-long learner"?
3. Think of some encouraging words that will inspire you for the future.

Writing

Imagine that you are one of the speakers at Luz's career night.
Write a short summary of your speech.

Be sure to include:

- a brief description of your career and how you got started in it
- the career ladder from entry level to more advanced
- where you are now in your career
- what you like and dislike about your career
- advice or lessons learned

Skill building: job applications & resumés

1. Collecting your personal information is the first step to writing a resumé. This will also be useful in completing paper and online job applications.

2. The resumé describes your skills and gives specific information about what you did on the job.

3. The application or resumé is often the first impression an employer has of you. It is the first thing that "sells" you for the job.

4. In preparing to write your resumé, refer to discussions of your strengths and likes from Unit 1.

Using skills

Complete the resumé worksheet, and/or any job application you have.

RESUMÉ WORKSHEET

Name _____

Address _____

City, State, Zip _____

Phone _____

Email _____

Job Objective: _____

Skills and Experience:

Employment:
(dates (most recent first), title, organization, email/phone, job responsibilities)

Education:
(name of school, location, course of study, dates)

References (3):
On a separate page, include name, title, phone or email.

Research

Choose a topic that is of interest to you because you want to find out more information about it. This is your final research project. This project should be something that will help you further your career and education goals. It will help you narrow your choices, eliminate those that won't work for you, and possibly open new doors of opportunity.

Here are some examples:

1. Research apprenticeships available for green jobs. Find out the answers to questions about qualifications and availability.

2. Investigate how to start a small business and get loans. Find out about Small Business Administration loans; further develop your business plan. Consider the pros and cons of your choices.

3. Explore the viability of a cooperative in your community. Get information about licensing, credentials, insurance, budgeting, and management.

4. Research admissions and financial aid at a university. Talk to a student advisor, go to an orientation session, and compile information.

5. Look into the various organizations that employ nursing assistants (GNA and CNA). Investigate the potential for growth each of the places offers. Consider a project to define the necessary requirements for LPN and RN, and places where you can go for those degrees.

Now, choose YOUR project and present it in a power point, speech, paper, or whatever way best describes what you have learned. Share with the other students so that we can all learn.

Remember the career exploration websites from Unit 2? These will help:

> www.acinet.org/acinet/explore/View.aspx
> www.careerinfonet.org

Final Writing Reflection

Answer the following question: What have you learned in class that will help you achieve your goals or dreams?

Resources

http://eff.cls.utk.edu/PDF/WorkReadinessProfile.pdf

http://n8tip.com/the-hamburger-method-of-constructive-criticism-works-for-vegetarians-too

http://sixthinkinghats.com/

www.acinet.org/acinet/explore/View.aspx

www.ahlei.org/

www.americanprogress.org/issues/green/report/2009/04/06/5844/a-green-jobs-primer/www.careercc.com/interv3.shtml

www.careerinfonet.org

www.collegeboard.com/student/testing/accuplacer/accuplacer-tips.html

www.eslpartyland.com/teachers/conversation/cqtech.htm

www.executive-and-life-coaching.com/support-files/smartgoalsettingworksheet.pdf

www.gttp.org/html/canadalinks/curriculum/AppdxA.htm – Canadian Travel and Tourism 5 Steps to Solving a Problem

www.indeed.com/forum/job/Computer-Technician/best-computer-technician-qualifications-training-get/t6643

www.microsoft.com/learning/student-career/en/us/career-job-role-chart.aspx

www.microsoft.com/learning/education/roadmap/

www.nc-net.info/ESL/guide.php (ESL Virtual Library of Lesson Plans)

www.nelrc.org/changeagent (September 2009 issue pages 50 and 51)

www.studydiscussions.com/how-to-choose-a-career-in-hospitality-industry/

www.testprepreview.com/modules/sentencecorrectiont.htm

www.virtualsalt.com/crebook2.htm

Glossary

A

to abuse - to treat a person badly   30

to accept - to take on, to agree to do something   1

administrator -   a manager of an organization   37

to advance - to move forward (to a new job)   1

appearance - the way someone or something looks   45

appliance - a piece of equipment, usually electric, for use in the home   18

to apply - to make a request for   1

apprenticeship – an opportunity to learn by practical experience from a master of a trade   18

approved - okayed, gave the O.K.   52

architect - a person who designs large structures, buildings, etc.   18

to arrange - to make plans   52

audience - people watching and listening to a show, concert, movie, or speech   62

B

bankrupt - unable to pay debts   35

basics - fundamental information, most important   10

blueprints - a print and guide of a technical drawing or design   18

bricklayer - a person who uses bricks (blocks of hardened clay) for construction   18

bruise - a blue-purple mark on your skin that appears after hitting something   13

C

CPR - (cardiopulmonary resuscitation) the procedure for restarting breathing and circulation of the blood   13

cancer - a dangerous growth anywhere in the body that may spread to other parts of the body   10

carpenter - a person who builds or repairs wooden structures - houses, shelves,
cabinets, etc.   18

cast - plaster put on a broken part of the body to keep it from moving until it heals   13

challenging - testing someone's abilities   28

chaos - a situation in which everything is confused and nothing is happening in
an organized way   26

character - the special behavior and qualities of a person   5

chef - skilled cook or main cook   43

child care center - a place where children are taken care of during the day   52

client - a person who receives services   28

competitive - competing with (matching or exceeding) other similar salaries   45

to complain - to say that you are unhappy, not satisfied   1

composting - changing organic matter into soil for gardening   21

computer technician - a person skilled in operating and fixing computers   35

confidence - sure about one's abilities to succeed   55

consensus - agreement by everyone   28

conservation - management, protection, and care of nature   21

consistent - always happening in the expected way   55

to construct - to build   18

continuity - continuing over a long time without interruption or change   55

contractor - a person who agrees by signing a contract to furnish supplies
and perform work at a price   18

counselor - a person who advises another person officially or professionally   18

co-worker - someone who works with you   52

crisis - big trouble, major problem   18

crutches - used to assist walking, with a handgrips and rests for the arms   13

culinary - having to do with kitchen or cooking   43

customer - person who buys items or services   5

D

dead-end - with no exit, no chance for progress or success   62

to deceive - to lie to someone; not tell the truth   5

demanding - requiring much time, effort, and attention   45

dementia - loss of mental powers   10

demolition - destruction of a building   30

to demonstrate - to show   52

determined - very motivated to be successful   1

diplomacy - skill in relations and dealing with people   5

disaster - a sudden event, an accident, flood or storm, that causes great harm or damage   35

discipline - to control behavior, obeying rules   55

discrimination - treat people differently because of prejudice   30

E

eager - ready and willing to go   62

ecstatic - showing great pleasure, feeling extremely happy   62

elderly - old people   1

electrician - a person who works in the construction, repair or installation (putting in) of electrical wiring   1

elementary - basic   62

emotional - having strong feelings   62

engineer - a professional who operates, plans, and services something   37

environment - surroundings; often refers to natural surroundings   18

eventually - at some later time   1

to exceed - to be more than   45

excited - energized, anticipating a happy feeling   52

expectations - hopes and desires, what you think should happen   26

expenditure - money or another asset spent or used up on something   21 *expenses* - the money spent to buy or to do something   5

to explore - to look at and think about something carefully   55

to export - to sell and send goods to another country   35

F

facility - something built to service specific purposes   45

family childcare centers - are usually in people's homes   52

finance - the management of money and other assets   26

to flee - to leave something quickly to escape danger   26

folks - people (informal)   52

to fracture - to break or crack   13

fuel - any material, such as coal, oil, gas, or wood, used to heat or give power   18

G

geek - someone very interested in computers and technology   37

geriatric - concerning the elderly   10

glazier - a person who installs glass, often in windows and doors   18

goal - something you want to accomplish   1

H

harmony - balance, agreement, fitting well together   18

hazard - danger   30

hazardous - dangerous and unsafe   21

to highlight - to draw attention to the best part   37

I

IT - computer data processing   37

increasing - making larger   52

independent - able to operate alone, not relying on others 30

initiative - the ability to think and act on your own, without being told 45

to install - to put onto or to put in 18

instinctive - done naturally without having to think about it 55

to integrate - to make something fit in with a group, or make whole 30

to interact - to communicate to others and work together with them 55

intern - someone in training to get experience 37

intrigued - interested 55

L

laid off - fired because of a company's financial difficulties 35

landscaping - designing the land by planting trees and flowers 21

leadership - ability to direct people 28

lodging - a place to live in, especially temporarily 45

to long - to feel a strong desire for something 52

M

maintenance - work that is necessary to keep something in good condition 26

majority - a greater number of people 65

to manage - to direct people, handle something, like in a business 5

manipulatives - objects used with your hands for exploration and learning 55

medication - the use of medicine to treat a disease or illness 10

merchandise - things that are for sale in stores 26

moved - touched deeply with feelings 52

N

nutritious - providing nutrition (food that is necessary to live and grow) 10

O

an obligation - a duty or agreement that has to be done 65

observations - carefully watching and learning from something you noticed 55

obstacle - something that gets in the way and stops progress 65

operating system - the main computer program that controls files and devices 37

opportunity - a chance to do something 26

to optimize - to making something work in the best way; fast and correct 63

options - choices 45

oral - spoken 37

P

patients - people who receive care 10

permanent residency - visa status that allows a person to live and work in the U.S. 26

personality - distinctive qualities of a person 45

photographic memory - the ability to remember things perfectly 37

plumber - a person who puts in and fixes pipes, and fixtures related to the water supply and drainage 18

to ponder - to think about very carefully 62

to pollute - to make dirty, corrupt, contaminate 18

to postpone - to change an event to a later time or date 35

precipitation - rain or snow 21

prep cook - a person who prepares food for the cook to use 43

to preserve - to make sure something is protected and kept safe 21

pulse - the regular beating of the heart felt in the arteries 13

to pursue - to chase or to work toward (a goal) 65

Q

quality - a characteristic of a person or thing   45

R

to raise - to take care of children until they are adults   35

reference - a person who is willing to speak about your skills and character to future employers   43

registered - qualified formally or officially by an institution   52

registered nurse - a nurse who is licensed by the state to practice nursing   10

to regret - sadness you feel about something you have done and wish you had not done   26

to reject - to not accept   1

relationship - a connection between two beings   5

relieved - comforted, calmed, not worried   13

to repair - to fix, to restore to good condition

requirement - something that is necessary to do   52

to restore - to put back into use   21

retirement community - a place where the elderly are taken care of   1

to retrofit - to change something by adding new parts to improve the way it works   21

rewarding - valuable, satisfying   5

S

senior staff - workers with a higher status   52

skill - ability, something a person is good at doing   1

software - the programs that tell a computer how to do a particular job   35

solar panels - panels that convert sunlight to electricity; often put on roofs of buildings   18

splint - a piece of wood (or metal) used to keep a broken bone in place   13 *splinter* - a sharp, thin piece of wood   13

stitches - thread used to close a wound   13

stock - items needed to keep for future sales   5

to store - to place or leave something (food) somewhere (refrigerator)   43

strategies - plans carefully developed to meet a goal   18

stressful - full of or causing tension, unrest, imbalance   43

success - a satisfactory outcome, good results, something works out well   10

supplies - items needed for a task   5

T

temper - sudden anger   5

terminal illness - an illness that ends in death   10

thrive - to become healthy in mind and body   55

toddler - young child, usually learning to walk   52

toxic - having a poison that causes harm or death   21

to transfer - to move from one place or situation to another   45

troubled - worried (unhappy) or anxious (not able to relax)   1

to troubleshoot - to deal with serious problems, to investigate   35

tweezers - small pincers for pulling out hairs, small objects, or splinters   13

typically - normally, usually   45

U

unconscious - not being able to feel or think   13

to upgrade - to raise to a higher level, to add new knowledge   1

V

valid - officially acceptable 52

vital signs - physical signs that show one is alive - heartbeat, breathing, temperature, blood pressure 10

W

wages - money paid to an employee 28

weatherization - protection from cold weather 21

welder - a person who heats material to get it to fuse together 18

widow - a woman whose husband has died and who has not married again 35

wise - having knowledge, showing good judgment 10

to wonder - to consider something without being sure about it 1

to worry - to think about someone or something a lot due to feeling nervous 43

wound - an injury to the body in which the skin is broken, cut, or torn 13

Y

to yell - to shout or say something very loudly 43